I0422168

The Outdoor Prepper

Using Your Landscape for Survival

By Joe Wild

© 2015

All rights reserved. No part of this publication may be reproduced, distributed, or transmitted in any form or by any means, including photocopying, recording, or other electronic or mechanical methods, without the prior written permission of the publisher, except in the case of brief quotations embodied in critical reviews and certain other non-commercial uses permitted by copyright law.

Are You Prepared? To Survive in the Great Outdoors?

You know you need to be prepared. But maybe you don't know where to start? Maybe you consider yourself an expert prepper already. Maybe you're just a beginner. But are you ready to live outdoors? To survive away from your home? No matter how long you've been prepping, we all make mistakes. It's natural. It's human. And mistakes happen more often when you are living outside your comfort zone. But there are ways you can learn from others and avoid the same mistakes that we all make.

With this book, you'll learn how to be prepared to live outdoors, off of the land, and to survive for as long as you need to!

If you are interested in learning how to protect your family from any and all of the inevitable disasters that could potentially happen, this book is your first step to learning how to prepare for any emergency situation and how to survive in the great outdoors.

Don't wait - Get started today!

The Outdoor Prepper: *Using Your Landscape for Survival*

Skilled preppers augment their homes for security and survival. In fact, most preppers will tell you that your home is one of the most important resources you'll have in a disaster. The types of disasters we anticipate vary. Some of us fear natural events, and others are certain that governments will eventually fall, and anarchy will reign.

Regardless of our individual notions of threats to our security, in preparation, many of us have carefully stocked storage rooms full of canned food, bottled water, and other household supplies. We may even have locked and scrupulously maintained weaponry, and garages full of generators, fuels, and hand tools. Still, some disasters, not too far beyond the imagination, have the potential to affect the security of even the most prepared home.

Natural disasters such as avalanches, earthquakes, tsunamis or fires can wipe out everything in a flash. Roads could become impassable. Electricity and communications could go down. Fresh water systems, and food security may be curtailed. In a time of warfare, homes might be requisitioned, or even invaded. Although we hope and pray to never experience such disastrous circumstances, it is sensible to be prepared.

In the event that your home becomes insecure and you are required to leave quickly, or are otherwise blocked from your home, you need to know where you can go, and which resources are useful and available in your region. This guide intends to help you prepare for short-term use of the landscape in your area for shelter or escape.

This is not a homesteading guide, but I will draw on some important homesteading techniques in this discussion. Also, while I will refer to some devices that require batteries or fuel, I will not give you a shopping list of tech devices you need to buy. Instead, I want to show you how you can be prepared even if phones, cars, radios, and etc. all shut down. Remember, we cannot predict the course of events, but we can prepare to survive regardless.

Part 1: Assessing Your Landscape

The first step in preparing to abandon your home, or to cope if you can't reach home, is assessing your landscape. Natural land and water features provide secure shelter, routes for escape, and sustenance, but first you have to discover the world outside your door through careful and conscientious exploration. Begin by taking stock of your prior knowledge. How well do you know the roads, pathways, parks, watercourses, and other important aspects of the landscape in your region? Here are the top five questions you should be able to answer about your region:

Five Essential Questions

1. Can you reach a natural shelter or partial shelter safely and within a reasonable time period?
2. How close to your home is the nearest source of fresh water?
3. Which edible plants grow in your area?
4. Are there wild animals in your area?
5. Are there alternative routes of escape nearby, in the event that your original plan is compromised, or you are being pursued?

Later, I will provide you with more information about each of these questions. For now, your goal is to take inventory of what you already know about the natural environment around your home.

Once you have a sense of your prior knowledge, it's time to explore the unfamiliar.

I suggest you begin your regional explorations with a series of carefully planned day hikes. The purpose of the hikes is to discover how far you need to travel from your home before your reach natural habitat, and then to take stock of the features in that area.

For our purposes we will consider a 'natural habitat' to be any area that is not part of the urban or suburban built environment. A local park, or a farmer's field may contain vital resources in a time of crisis. If you are too far from a natural habitat to walk to it, you should plan alternative transportation, such as bicycles or ATVs, in the event that roads are closed. You should conduct day hikes regularly, and in more than one direction, learning all you can. Consider as many scenarios as you can imagine.

For example: if a fire is burning south of your home, where will travelling directly north lead you? What if you are injured, and you cannot travel more than a few miles? Keep in mind that an average walking speed is approximately 3 mph.

Your physical condition will greatly impact how effectively you implement an on-foot escape plan, as well as your ability to survive away from the comforts of home. Record your plan for the hikes, and you findings each time you return. Keeping a log is one small way to organize and maintain your preparedness.

If you will be exploring particularly remote or challenging terrain, you might consider using an ATV, as this will allow you t travel further, and faster. Keep in mind that speed is not always an advantage in the bush. You goal is to observe and record. So, if you are not walking, make frequents stops to scan the ground, foliage, water, and horizon.

Bicycles may be used, but in some terrains they will be more of an obstacle than an aid. Also, if you cycle quickly, be careful that the silence of your approach doesn't startle wildlife. It is one thing to scare a flock of partridge from a shrub, but entirely another to whip silently around a corner and ride directly into the path of a mountain lion.

It is vitally important to feel confidently familiar with your landscape, so that when you need to use it, you will already know what to expect.

Making a Record

You'll want to create a knowledge base of information about your surroundings, either for yourself, or for your family in the event that you are separated. Create a *regional resources guidebo*ok by photographing, or illustrating key features and locations in your area. Remember, in some disaster scenarios, you will be unable to rely on your telephone and Internet devices for information.

Make a portable, hard copy book (using any of the popular apps like Shutterfly ™ or Montage ™) by recording vital landscape information and images. Photographs of edible plants, and maps showing important lookout points or hiding places may serve you, or someone you love well in a crisis. Your guidebook might also contain copies of important documents such as birth, marriage and death certificates, property ownership and insurance papers, and your last will and testament.

I suggest making multiple copies of your custom guide and keeping one in every vehicle (including boats), in your home, and in your wilderness cache. More on wilderness caching below!

Pro Tip: Keep a notebook and pencil on your person at all times. When you discover new information, or recall and important tip or idea, just jot it down. Use this notebook to supplement you regional resources guidebook.

So, what are you looking as you explore your landscape? Good question! Thinking about our five key questions from the introduction of this article, we can break down the goals for our exploration into 3 main categories: shelter, sustenance, and travel routes. We will also take quick look at some other wilderness skills like signaling and crafting.

Remember, we need to consider survival first. There are many ways to supplement and improve upon the suggestions you will find here, but I want to give you a starting point for making use of your landscape.

Shelter

Shelter is likely the first concern you will have in the event of a disaster that separates you from your home. Shelter provides protection from the elements, and predators. It is also necessary because even in the worst imaginable situation, people need to rest and restore calm thinking. Without secure shelter around us, it is very difficult for your body and mind to relax and gather strength, let alone sleep. So your plans for shelter are paramount.

We are going to discuss 3 types of shelters:

1. Pre-existing shelters
2. Shelters utilizing landscape features
3. Tents

Pre-existing Shelters

Caves or pits do exist in some natural landscapes and may provide excellent short-term shelter, but they *are rare* and often already inhabited by wildlife! Use caution when approaching any natural outdoor shelter. If you are lucky enough to have a cave or underground pit near your home, you may want to secure it for future use by barricading the entrance with natural materials.

This will prevent any unwanted surprises from bears, snakes, or worse! (Actually, what could be worse than snakes?) In some regions, there may be mine shafts in your landscape. These can be exceptionally useful, but again, use caution. You will want to assess the structural soundness of any cave, pit, or shaft you enter. Look for supports around and above the shelter. Tree roots surrounding the interior of a cave provide excellent support, and are a good signal that the walls and ceiling are sound.

If you are investigating a natural or manmade pit as a possible shelter, you must also consider water-run off. Is there a way to redirect water from the pit entrance? If not, you should probably abandon that site. It is unlikely that a dry, safe cave can be reached by walking from your home into the wilderness, but natural habitats provide other options to keep you dry and warm.

Sheltering oneself among tree branches is hardly an ideal choice for survival, but taking to the tress may be your only choice if you are being stalked, or otherwise unable to sleep on the ground. If you must climb a tree to find safety, move slowly and carefully. Once you have balanced yourself in as secure a position as possible, use rope from your kit to secure yourself to the tree. Needless to say, unless you plan to build a tree house (not a bad idea actually), this is only a temporary shelter solution.

Pro Tip: *Bears, mountain lions, and other predators can all climb trees, much better than humans can even. Don't think you'll be safe just by scurrying up a tree!*

Shelters Using the Landscape: Lean-tos and Tarp Shelters

Lean-tos and tarps can be easily rigged up next to hillocks, large rocks, cliffs, or between trees. Buy good quality tarps that have grommets. They are slightly more expensive, but securing them will be much easier. Also, you should have tarps in a variety of colors: neutral brown and green to camouflage your site, and red or blue to signal for help or attract others to your camp.

*Pro Tip: While setting up a tent or tarp under or between trees is a convenient way to utilize nature, remember that you need to **move away from tall trees in a lightning storm**. Find an open area and crouch as low as you can until the storm passes.*

Here are a few suggestions for how to erect a sturdy lean-to using either tarps or natural materials. First, try to locate your lean-to adjacent to a natural support, such as a rock wall, a stand of trees, or a steeply sloping hillside. Don't forget to ensure that water will run out of, not into, your shelter.

The natural feature forms the back wall of your shelter. Ideally, the front or entrance of your shelter should not face directly into the wind. Depending on your region, you may have easy access to wood fall. If so, lean large branches or poles against the back 'wall', and secure them with ropes or by lodging the ends of each pole into the soil or between stones. Finally, proceed to either stretch and secure your tarp across the branches, or find natural materials to 'thatch' your lean-to.

Again depending on your region, you may use straw, reeds, palm leaves, evergreen branches, bamboo, or grasses. Regardless of which natural material you choose, remember to keep your fire a good distance away!

Pro Tip: *Keeping fire away from your newly built shelter is critical, but you also want to keep your sanitation area (toilet!) down slope and well away from where you will sleep and cook. Also, you should never defecate anywhere near your source of fresh water.*

Tents

You can purchase tents to suit almost any condition or landscape, but there are some key considerations in making your choice. Think about the capacity, weather resistance, weight, and difficulty of assembly of the tent you plan to purchase.

There is a great deal of difference between a backpacking or tent (which could be ideal for your go-bag), and a camping tent that likely has more features, but is far less portable. If you are planning shelter for more than just one individual you may want to purchase numerous tents in a variety of sizes.

Tents are also categorized according to their weather capacity. Three season tents are intended for spring, summer and early autumn camping, while a four-season tent will see you through the winter. Choose a tent based on the prevailing climate in your region. If your landscape is covered with snow and ice for more than 30 days a year, it would be foolhardy to depend upon a tent intended for summer camping.

Also, consider how you will be carrying your tent to your shelter location. Travelling straight uphill? You will want to choose a tent made of the lightest possible materials, such as hollow aluminum tubing and nylon, as opposed to steel and canvas!

Finally, and this is very important, practice setting up your tent at least once. In a real crisis, you may be in a hurry to escape the elements, and you'll be grateful that you don't have to stop and read the instructions.

Shelters Using the Landscape: Rocks

It's unlikely you'll want to use rocks to build shelter for a short-term stay. However, if the situation dictates a prolonged time in the outdoors, rocks can be excellent for making walls, storage spaces, and fire pits.

Pro Tip: The purpose of a fire pit is to keep your fire from spreading to your campsite or into nearby brush. A fire pit also helps to concentrate heat for cooking. Make your fire pit small enough that you can keep it burning, but large enough that you don't have to cut wood into inconveniently small pieces for fuel.

There are a few basic considerations for building anything out of rocks. Assuming rocks are available in your area, and you are able to lift and place them, the following rules will help you build solid structures that are unlikely to collapse. First, always build upwards with the largest and heaviest rocks on the bottom.

Secondly, assess each rock to determine which side of it is the weightiest. For example, a rock that is roughly the shape of a scalene triangle will have one side that carries most of the weight. This is the side that should press most directly downward. Weight that tips off to one side of your structure will eventually slide!

Another way to prevent sliding is to have the maximum amount of the rocks' surface areas touching each other. You can mortar a simple rock wall with just about anything, from small stones and mud to grass or leaves, but friction and weight are the true secrets to a sturdy rock wall. Another thing to keep in mind is the width vs. the height of your wall.

As a rough rule, for every foot of height, you should have at least six inches of width. In other words, a five-foot hand-built rock retaining wall should be approximately two and a half feet wide. Before sleeping next to your rock structure, test it to make sure it is safe. You should be able to lean against it, sit on top of it, and pour water over it without any movement or shifting of stones.

Pro Tip: *Building with heavy rocks? Keep those clever Egyptians in mind! They used levers to move massive rocks great distances. You can move rocks as big as 100bs on your own if you have the right tools: a pole and a fulcrum, but please, practice with something smaller first!*

A Final Word about Shelter

Now that you know some of your options for shelter in a crisis, you should consider which locations will suit your needs best. Moving to higher ground is often advisable. As you ascend a mountain or hillside, you will be more difficult to pursue on foot. A higher location also provides the opportunity to survey your surroundings.

However, you do have to get all of your gear up the hill with you, and wind and weather can be considerably worse at higher locations. Still, it's important to stay near water, and downhill is generally a better direction for seeking ground water or another fresh water source.

On the other hand, low-lying areas present higher risks in particular natural disaster scenarios, such as earthquake and tsunami. Your best chance of survival is to prepare for two or three different locations that suit different circumstances. Describe and map them carefully in your *regional resources guidebook,* and make sure everyone in your family knows how to reach these locations in an emergency.

It is also a good idea to establish one or two 'rally points' within a reasonable distance of your shelter sites. Rally points are locations where your group can assemble if separated. Generally speaking, your rally point provides a safety net that protects your shelter and cache from unwanted intruders.

Should a member of your group arrive at the rally point with an unknown or unwelcome individual (for example: in a hostage situation), your survival site will not have necessarily been compromised.

Sustenance: Food and Water

Every prepper knows that food and water are primary considerations for survival, but did you know that many landscapes are surprisingly good sources of nutrition and hydration in an emergency? Getting to know the plants and animals that inhabit your region is not only smart, but it could save your life.

Ubiquitous plants like clover, dandelions, chickweed, and even seaweed, are edible and will give your body the energy it needs to keep warm, hydrated, and to hunt for more protein-rich food sources. Many colorful flower petals are edible (but bitter tasting). Plant roots provide some of the tastier and more nutritious wilderness food options. Prolific plants like Cattails and Joe Pye Weed have roots that may be eaten raw or boiled.

5 Tips for Harvesting and Eating Wild Plants

1. If you don't know what it is, don't' eat it.
2. Take only branches or leaves, do not kill the whole plant. If it proves tasty, you may want to use it again.
3. Wash your hands and the plant before you try any type of preparation.
4. Sample the plant raw, in a 'salad'.
5. Make the plant into a tea!

Pro Tip: *The seeds of a pine tree are edible and provide nutrition in an emergency! Calorie and vitamin E rich, pine nuts are tricky to harvest, but worth the trouble if you're in trouble. Find this food in the wing-shaped interior of pinecones. The nuts are inside very hard shell casings. DO NOT to try and bite the shells open. Instead use a rock, or hammer if one is handy.*

Most healthy birds, mammals, and even insects are edible, but you need to have the strength and wit to catch and prepare them.

Birds are not easy to catch or hunt, but here are a few suggestions to get you started. Birds like berries! Check your landscape, and if there are naturally occurring berry bushes, such as huckleberries or blueberries, birds won't be too far off. A slingshot is one of the easier hunting tools to make with a y-shaped branch.

Some websites suggest using rubber surgical tubing for the sling, but a thick elastic or flat shock cord will work as well. If you are a hunter, sinew is the strongest material you can use to secure the sling. If not, twine or even dental floss works too!

Fish and shellfish are also important sources of food in wilderness survival. A rudimentary fishing lure is easy to pack and assemble in the wilderness. Keep a small bag of hooks, line, and a sealed container of chemical bait in your pack and you're ready to go. Gather shellfish, such as clams and mussels, and remember to keep them alive until you are ready to eat them.

Don't assume that you will figure out how to catch a rabbit in an emergency. Hunting and fishing are activities that require skill, and that possess risks. Practice is the only way to ensure that you can feed yourself and your family in a crisis. Animal foods can be dangerous if not consumed immediately, so be sure to also learn all you can about processing and preserving meats and fishes as part of your preparation and planning.

Smoking, drying, and caning are just some of the methods for preserving foods and it's great to know a bit about each of these skills as well.

Water is without a doubt one of the most important considerations in a survival plan. In North America, individuals use between 50 and 100 gallons of water a day, for drinking, sanitation, cooking, and washing! Dehydration is a serious threat, and occurs much more quickly than you may think.

When we become dehydrated, systems in our bodies, including our major organs, begin to shut down, and often it is the capacity to reason that is first disabled, making it even harder for you to seek water. You must make yourself aware of the location of fresh water sources in your area.

Consult maps, but also look for rushes, cattails, or reeds that typically grow in and around water. The presence of mud and buzzing insects are also good clues that a source of water is nearby. Scan hillsides for deeply cut valleys, because this is where you'll find brooks, streams, or rivers.

Fortunately, many water filtering systems and tablets are on the market. Boiling water, or purifying it with tablets or filtering is essential. Fresh water carries thousands of organisms, and many of them can make you critically ill. Also, if the only water source available is ice or snow, it's important to melt it before you drink. Otherwise, it will only increase your dehydration by reducing your body temperature.

Water testing kits can be purchased online, and in some hardware stores, but if you are relying on a natural, unprocessed water source, finding a purification method is not optional. If you are extremely dehydrated, you must rehydrate slowly to avoid shocking your system. Take small sips over a long period of time, until you begin to feel strong.

Pro Tip: *Groundwater is water that resides in the water table or aquifers. Although difficult to locate and extract, in a disaster this water is the least likely natural source of water to be contaminated. Add knowledge about groundwater to your research priority list.*

Personal hygiene is another important consideration for survival in the wilderness. Toileting, hunting, eating, and building shelter in the wilderness will result in illness and even disease if you do not keep clean.

Portable, disinfecting wet wipes, and waterless hand cleaners are enormously useful if you are able to pack and or cache them (other cache supplies are covered in the next section). If you have suffered an injury, and have an open wound, being in the wilderness place you in grave danger of infection. Keep all wounds scrupulously clean and bandaged if at all possible.

Women's hygiene presents particular wilderness challenges. Your caches and packs should contain supplies for women in your party. The best option for most menstruating women is a washable menstrual cup.

Disposable pads and tampons are just not sensible in the outdoors. In an emergency, moss is useful as an absorbent material. Finally, the legend that bears are attracted to menstrual blood has been largely disproved. Still, staying as clean as possible is always a good plan.

Collecting Resources and Tools

If you are planning for an escape into a natural environment, there are a few tools that are essential to have on hand. Remember, in a real emergency or disaster scenario, there may not be time to rush around your home collecting these items. Keep them in a go-bag or kit, ready to pick up and run with at any time. Some people keep go-bags in numerous locations: cars, campers, cottages, and boats. If you can afford the expense, this level of preparation is advisable.

Top Ten Tools for Emergency Situations

Note: There are many lists like mine available on the Internet. You may want to adjust your list according to your region, family size, or other considerations.

1. Knife
2. Tarp
3. Hatchet and Wedge
4. Fire Starting Kit
5. Rope
6. Boots and Gloves
7. Metal, Watertight Pot or Bucket
8. Compass
9. Candles
10. First Aid Kit

11.

*Note: This list doesn't include food and water! But you need those too. See below.

> **Pro Tip**: *Chicken wire is a surprisingly versatile, and portable emergency item. This lightweight material may be used to block the opening to your shelter or cache, or to create a sturdier frame for a tent or tarp. It even provides a rudimentary grill surface for a wood fire.*

Essential Foodstuffs

While eating plants and animals found in the landscape may be possible, it is a good idea to have some food and water ready to take with you if time and conditions permit. What you pack will depend partly on personal taste, but try to include high energy, long lasting, and versatile items. You should always have enough food on hand to feed yourself and your family for a minimum of three days. Here are my top ten picks for your bug-out food pack.

Top Ten Foods for an Emergency Survival Kit

1. Flour
2. Peanut Butter
3. Soup Stock
4. Dried Fruit
5. Canned Fish, Meat, or Poultry
6. Sugar and Salt
7. Dried pulses (lentils, chickpeas, etc.)
8. Honey
9. Rice
10. Powdered Milk

This is by no means a definitive list. I would probably add candy and chocolate to my pack, and I'm sure there are others who can't imagine survival without coffee!

You can supplement with as much as you carry. Also, many outdoor suppliers carry survival foods such as freeze dried meals and snacks. However, this is often a pricey way to prepare for an emergency, and some products may be overly salty and otherwise bland. It's easy to pack a few dried herbs and spices, and add them to your basics to create the flavors you prefer without all the expense.

Another thing to keep in mind is that hiking and building shelter will make you ravenous. Even if you are normally a light eater at home, you need extra fuel for your body when you are in the great outdoors. It's colder, for one thing, and food provides critical energy to keep you warm.

Pro Tip: *Humans have been cooking bread over fires since time immemorial. You can do it with just self-rising flour, water, and a little salt. Make dough using about 1 cup of the flour, 2/3 cup of water, and a ¼ teaspoon of salt. Mash it into a flat shape. Drape it over a hot stone and cook on your fire! Yum!*

Getting Away: Identifying Escape Routes

In ideal circumstances, when disaster strikes, we will all jump in our SUVs and drive off into the sunset. However, in a crisis we may not be able to use vehicles or roads. That's why you should know about natural pathways and other possible routes away from danger. We will look at two types of escape routes: land and water.

Routes Over Land

Pre Existing Land Routes: Hiking Trails, Power Lines, Train Tracks and Resource Roads

Wherever man interferes in a natural landscape you will likely find some route or path leading away from a main road and into the bush. Hiking trails are the most obvious of these, but may not be enormously useful during an emergency because it's likely many people will attempt to use such routes.

However, knowing where such trails are located is a good idea. Most city, state and national parks publish maps of maintained hiking or walking trails that you can request for free. This is probably the easiest reconnaissance you can do because park trails are maintained, and may have fully operational facilities like outhouses, stocked fire pits, and picnic sites.

Take the family along and enjoy the great outdoors, while observing the area for its emergency potential.

Power transmission lines, the large towers that move electricity from power generating centers into cities and towns, cut wide avenues through natural environments in many parts of North America and Europe. These corridors are generally kept clear of overgrown bush to allow access for repair.

For this reason, they make particularly good roadways for ATVs. Find out where the power line routes closest to you are located, and learn about the area they traverse. Remember that these towers **transmit powerful electric current** and therefore you should never attempt to climb them, or use them as part of your shelter plans.

Train tracks also crisscross many natural landscapes in almost all parts of the world. The advantages to following train tracks are that they typically follow a reasonable grade, so you won't be hefting your gear up particularly steep inclines. Also, if you are lost, following a train track will take you to a community of some sort, where you may find help or at least supplies.

Another consideration is that train tracks are frequently maintained by crews of workers. Inevitably, those workers leave debris and potentially supplies along their route. You may be lucky enough to find a forgotten cache if you stick to the tracks.

Also, you can ride a bicycle on well-maintained tracks, and in some areas even abandoned tracks are used so frequently for this purpose that you may find them passable. Consider purchasing a bike trailer if this might be an option for you.

Pro Tip: *As one of our earliest forms of mass transportation, trains are likely to be one of the last still operating after a crisis as well. Never walk on tracks while wearing earplugs, buds or headphones.*

Pay attention to vibrations, and rest at least 15 feet from the tracks to avoid danger.

Miners and loggers created webs of remote roadways throughout landscapes in their quest for natural resources. Unlike train tracks, these potential routes can be incredibly hazardous (think switchbacks, ice roads, and avalanche danger).

However, a resource road is sometimes preferable to raw bush depending on your circumstances. These routes may take you to an abandoned or recently operational worksite. If so, you could come upon critical supplies or even shelter.

Still, many of these roads are now totally desolate, pockmarked with potholes, strewn with deadfall, and any evidence that people once worked on or near them is long gone. Don't count on a resource route to take you to civilization, as many of them end, literally, in the middle of nowhere.

Natural Land Routes

Did you know that even in completely uninhabited areas it's possible to find well-worn paths leading to safety and water? If you are familiar with animal tracking, this is probably not news. Certainly, there are many manmade hiking trails in natural landscapes, but animals of many kinds also create paths through wilderness areas.

You will be able to recognize these paths by learning more about the creatures that live in your area. Study their tracks (footprints!), scat (poop!), and other signs of animals passing, such as broken tree limbs, patches of flattened grass or moss, and fur stuck to shrubs or branches.

Following trails left by animals comes with some risk, but probably less risk than setting off into dense bush, forest, tundra, or desert without any sense of where you might be going. Like you, animals need food and water! Staying in or close to areas where animals travel is a good bet for a safe escape.

Another excellent tactic for choosing a land route is to stay on land but close by a waterway. This serves a couple of purposes. Rivers and streams provide food and water, and so long as you stay near the waterway, you won't have to do without either.

Another advantage of staying near water is that often waterways offer sound cover. If you need to travel with some stealth, a rushing river will disguise any noises that you or your party might make.

Pro Tip: *Even though a river can drown out some sounds, remember that voices carry great distances. This is particularly the case over still or slow moving water. If you don't want to be heard, don't make noise at the edge of lakes or other quiet bodies of water.*

Water Routes

Travelling on water is another way to put distance between yourself and danger, but you really need to have some knowledge of weather and water safety to put this plan into practice. Whether your preferred watercraft is a canoe, sailing dory, or 40 ft. power launch, know your boating and water safety practices before you proceed.

Rivers

Fast moving bodies of water, like rivers, are particularly dangerous. Unseen rocks, rapids, and debris impede progress, and in some areas animal predators abound. If crossing a river, look for places where rocks or log jams slow the current.

You will be surprised how quickly a current can knock you off balance, and how difficult it is to swim or stand against fast moving water. If you are in a canoe, or other watercraft in an unfamiliar river, stay close to the shore.

There may be more debris and obstacles near the shore, but your likelihood of being overturned, or surprised by rapids is much less. Rivers tend to go in only one direction - so make sure if you are using a river to escape danger that it is taking you in the direction you want to go!

Lakes

Lakes present altogether different types of dangers. You may set out on a lake in perfect weather and find blackening skies above you in a very short time. Again, staying near shore is advisable, and most certainly if you are paddling.

If your boat has a mast, you are at risk of lightening strikes, so pay attention to the sky. One final rule: if you are resourceful enough to have a boat, you should also have life jackets for everyone who boards her. Don't think that just *having* lifejackets is adequate preparation! You must be wearing your lifejacket when trouble strikes if you expect it to save your life!

A Word About Ice
In northern regions, and at high elevations, ice fishing, and snowmobiling are popular winter activities. In a disaster or crisis, an ice covered lake might seem to present an option for crossing a large distance quickly. Don't' make this mistake!

You must not attempt ice crossing unless you have extensive experience, know how to measure ice thickness, and have the safety gear necessary to attempt a rescue should that become be necessary. For one thing, in an escape scenario you will be loaded down with heavy gear.

Also, hypothermia sets in very quickly and is close to impossible to treat without medical attention. This type of travel route is likely not worth the risk, except in the most extreme circumstances.

Oceans

Unlike freshwater travel, using the ocean to travel or escape requires you to be informed about tides and navigation. It's *possible* to get lost on a lake, even a small one, but on the ocean it's almost guaranteed if you don't know what you are doing.

This is because tides and ocean currents play with boats like children's toys. In an ocean, you can think you are going in one direction, and quickly end up somewhere else entirely. If you are located near the ocean, I recommend taking a basic nautical navigation course to familiarize yourself with potentially life-saving techniques.

One advantage of nautical navigation is that it is possible to determine your location and plot a course without any electronic devices. Never heard of a sextant or seen a nautical chart? These are important tools for an ocean escape, and a course in nautical navigation will teach you what you should buy and what you need to know.

If you live near the ocean, you may already be familiar with the closest boat launch or marina, and if not, you should investigate.

Boat owners should also take boating safety courses as part of a licensing program. The skills you learn in such courses will apply and be useful to many aspects of survival planning.

If you are fortunate enough to own a boat, consider using it as an alternative cache site, and if your boat is engine driven, always have paddles on board for times when fuel is scarce or unobtainable. Travel by sail is a pre-modern technology that will be necessary when fuel sources and motorized vessels become scarce.

Pro Tip: *In general, sighting birds during ocean travel is a sign that land is not too far away. If navigation is failing you, follow birds and they will lead you to shore.*

Modern Day Navigation: Maps, Charts, Compasses and Global Positioning Systems

I cannot overemphasize the importance of having up-to-date physical, topographical and road maps of your area. I suggest you visit your local parks office, city hall, and an established marine supply store to source your maps.

There are maps and changes available on the Internet, but you want to be sure that you select only the most up-to-date and accurate. Choose your maps carefully, and then have them laminated to prevent water damage.

Maps used to navigate in water are called 'charts', and are also critical if you plan to sail, motor, or paddle to safety. If you have not used charts in the past, learn to read them. Charts use different symbols and systems of measurement than land maps.

One of the simplest and most useful instruments you will own is a compass. In fact, this is another item that you will want to own in multiples. Still, a compass is only useful if you know how to use it, and remember to teach every individual in your family as well. Every Boy Scout knows how to use one… do you?

Pro Tip: One smart way to get the whole family involved in learning about how to use a map and compass is by introducing them to the fun activity called geocaching! Turn survival lessons into an exciting treasure hunt, and everyone will want to get involved.

Global Position Systems, once only used by experts, are now ubiquitous. In fact, there are so many battery-operated portable GPS units on the market, that even the experts are baffled by choice. You will find devices with pre-loaded maps, altimeters, barometers, compasses, cameras, touch screens, route tracking, radio calling, and etc.

As amazing as all of this technology is, none of the amazing tools and apps for GPS will be useful to you if the batteries run out, or internet service is interrupted. There are some excellent, compact and portable fuel cell battery chargers available. By all means add a GPS to your emergency kit, but have a back up plan as well.

Reconnaissance and Practice in the Landscape

Team Exploration vs. Going it Alone

If you have a family or close friends who are involved in your prepping activities, it is advisable to include them in your exploration of the landscape. Not only is it safer to hike and explore in pairs or groups, but the more eyes and ears at work, the more accurate your observations will be.

Assign tasks to each group member: note-taking, photography, marking the path, etc. Having your group with you will accomplish two goals. Firstly, it will divide the work: each individual can focus on his own area of interest or expertise, and then later share what they have learned with the group.

Secondly, exploring as a group or pair will give you a sense of the personality dynamics among your peers. Most successful survival scenarios involve just the right alchemy of leadership, confidence, caution, and intellect. Some people are less suited to the challenges of surviving disaster, or coping in a crisis.

Practicing tasks like setting up a tent, or mapping a route, will reveal the character of your companions. I am NOT suggesting that you eject members from your survival group! On the contrary, your ability to detect weaknesses or areas for improvement, will allow you to work with your group and develop stronger communication mechanisms and interpersonal skills.

Encourage more timid members of your group to take small risks as you explore, and set tasks for the leaders in your group that will force them to ask for help! If you are a group leader, invite suggestions about your own conduct and planning.

There is not one among us who cannot improve. These may seem like small interventions, but when a crisis comes, they may well pay off with a more cohesive, and competent survival group dynamic.

Even children can be helpful explorers if you gear the extent of your activities accordingly. Have them collect plants, take photos, and mark the trail with colored ribbons. Keep the emphasis on learning, and fun! For children at least, prepping should be an activity about planning ahead, building confidence, and not about instilling fear!

If you do plan to set off into the wilderness alone, you need to **make a plan and share it with someone**. Your level of experience is of no consequence. Never set off into the wilderness alone unless you have informed a trusted person of your plans. Before any wilderness hike, follow these steps:

Five Steps to Prepare for a Wilderness Hike

1. Establish an estimated time frame and tell someone where you are going and when to expect you back. You may also suggest steps to be taken should you not return by the appointed time.

2. Dress appropriately, and prepare for unexpected weather changes (hat, comfortable shoes, layers, etc.).

3. Pack adequate food and water in a pack or bag.

4. Pack 2 or 3 basic safety items even for a short hike (knife, flashlight, matches, etc.)

5. Fully charge any battery-operated devices you plan to carry with you.

Remember, there are no prizes for taking unnecessary risks. Stay focused on the tasks you have set for yourself, and remain aware of your surroundings at all times.

Activities to Test your Mettle

One of the best ways to prepare for a crisis is to practice the skills you may need to survive. I am as guilty as anyone else of thinking that because *I read a book about* building a shelter, that I will have no problem actually doing it! In reality, the experience is often very different from what is expected, and may teach valuable lessons in the bargain. Every prepper should know these five critical skills for surviving in the wild.

Survival Skills - Top 5

1. Start a fire. Challenge yourself to start a fire under various challenging conditions (no matches, wet wood, wind, etc.). Your ability to start and maintain a fire will save your life, so make this skill a priority.

2. Build shelter. Try to accomplish this task using ONLY what you find in your landscape. Stay overnight! Assess the condition of your shelter in the morning, and ask yourself what should have been done differently. There's always room for improvement.

3. Gather wild food. I know you have a bologna sandwich in your backpack, but collect the items you would eat if you didn't. Once you are home again, identify each plant, research the nutritional value, flavor, and availability of the edible plants you selected, and animals or fish you harvested. Don't forget to record the information in your guidebook.

4. Travel by night. If danger comes in the form of other humans, you will want to be able to move through the landscape undetected. The best way to do this is to navigate using the stars. Here's one simple fact to help you find out which direction you are facing: stars appear to move across the sky from east to west!

5. Physical improvement. Your body will serve you well in the wilderness if exercise and practice activities like climbing, swimming and hiking. Demand a little more of yourself each time you explore your region.

Pro Tip: *Start a fire in windy conditions with ease by keeping a straw or small length of tubing in your pack. Place the tube into the center of your kindling pile and use your breath to direct a gentle stream of oxygen towards your spark.*

Wilderness Caching

One way to supplement your at-home stores, is to create a wilderness cache of emergency supplies. This is your PLAN B cache, so it should be a pared down version of whatever preparation you have done at home. Ideally, a wilderness cache should be located on your own property, and some preppers purchase wilderness acreage in part for this purpose.

Assuming you don't own property, you will want to choose a site far from frequently used trails. Many people record using National or State Parks, as they feel assured that no significant changes (like development) are likely to occur to these landscapes. Be discreet about the location you choose, and if you are using a GPS, mark your location digitally, as well as on a topographical or physical features map.

The most secure way to hide a cache is by burying it, and then disguising the area to appear undisturbed. Bury as deeply as you can manage, leaving at least four feet from the top of your cache to ground level. The size of the cache is up to you, but make sure that the container you choose is completely waterproof.

You also want to keep rodents, and insects from getting into your supplies. I have heard of caches stored in just about every container imaginable: Rubbermaid™ bins, PVC pipe, garbage cans, metal trunks, even repurposed toolboxes. Add extra waterproofing by running a bead of silicone along the sealed areas of your container before you bury it in the ground.

Your choice of container will be dictated by home much material you plan to cache. Draw from the lists presented earlier in this article, but consider the following items as well:

Wilderness Survival Cache – 20 Items that May Save Your Life

1. Bottled water (unopened bottled water can be stored for up to two years)
2. Easy to prepare foods.
3. Extra clothes, wet weather gear, boots and wool socks and caps
4. Flashlights and batteries (or hand crank lights)
5. Tent or Tarps
6. Maps
7. Emergency first aid supplies (bandages, pain medication, rubbing alcohol, anti-nausea medication, etc.)
8. Firearm and ammunition, or other method of self-defense like pepper spray or a sling shot
9. Communication device (CB, UHF or Ham radio)
10. Fire starting materials
11. Knives
12. Sleeping bags
13. Vitamins
14. Tobacco, coffee, other tradable goods
15. Fishing equipment
16. Flares
17. Copy of your *regional resources guidebook*
18. Whistle (for signaling – see below)
19. Camp stove and fuel

20. Unscented Chlorine Bleach (for disinfecting tools and purifying water from natural sources – 2 drops of bleach for every quart of water)

To securely store these items, place them in Ziploc or garbage bags as an additional water barrier. Place the heaviest items in the bottom of your cache container. You'll notice that some of the items listed here differ somewhat from what I recommended earlier for your go-bag. That's because your survival cache should be considered an absolute last resort.

This is a resource you will use when you are literally on the run, and it contains items that reflect an emerging or immediate threat. You may be injured, or escaping after a long period of being trapped or forcibly held somewhere. This type of cache provides immediate relief: water, food, warm clothes, and means of self-defense, should that become necessary.

Pro Tip: Even the toughest outdoorsmen can succumb to near madness at the tiny nuisance of biting and buzzing insects. A smoky fire is a natural deterrent, but keeping a good supply of repellant is also advisable.

It's understandable that you may want to talk about your preparations. Secrecy is not easy to maintain, but necessary. Try to resist the urge to brag about your emergency planning. A survival cache evokes intense curiosity in some folks, and it would be a shock to discover that someone looked for and broke into your supplies, no more so than in the moment you are relying on your pre-planning to save your life.

Signaling in the Landscape

SOS is the most universally recognized distress signal. Popular lore records that SOS stands for 'save our ship' or save our souls', but actually the letter combination was chosen because of its simplicity of use for Morse code, a system that uses dots and dashes in place of letters and numbers for communicating.

Nowadays, it's generally understood to mean 'people in distress, immediate aid required'. So, it could be a very handy signal to know how to use in an emergency. The audible version of SOS consists of three short tones, followed by three long and then three more short tones. These sounds are called 'dots and dashes' in Morse lingo.

You can mimic this pattern repeatedly in any number of ways: while chopping wood, by striking a metal container, or using a whistle. Similarly, you can leave SOS messages in the landscape in a variety of ways. If you are forced from your home and want to attract attention from rescuers, there are numerous ways to attract attention to your location, and indicate that you are in distress.

Use branches or stones to spell out SOS on a hillside, a beach, or an open field. You can spell out the letters or the symbols for dots and dashes - either will be recognizable. Overhead aircraft can easily spot manmade, symmetrical messages if they are large enough.

For radio users, the term 'Mayday' is a widely known distress signal, particularly within aeronautical and nautical organizations. Repeat this signal word three times in quick succession, and repeatedly, in a life threatening situation or emergency. Saying 'Mayday, Mayday, Mayday' ensures that the word is not misunderstood by listeners, and conveys the urgency of your situation.

Consider adding flares or a flare gun to your emergency supplies. This type of signal consists of a tube packed with explosives, much like fireworks, that can either be shot into the air, tossed into the water, or in some cases held onto. It is important to note that flares can themselves present serious dangers and hazards, and should only be used in pressing emergencies. Orange smoke flares are more typically recommended for daytime use, and red flares signal distress at night.

An air horn is an inexpensive item that you can buy in multiples and use to signal distress. These are compact, and the only risk they present is that children might get hold of them and damage their hearing. Used as directed by an adult, an air horn is a very effective way of getting attention.

If you are considering a signal fire, there are many instructional guides on how to build and maintain a fire over a period of time. However, remember that you may need the fuel used in a signal fire for heat and cooking, and it's critical to ration your resources carefully.

One very simple way of creating a signal using a fire is to set fire to a tree. Again, and I can't emphasize this enough, this type of distress signals comes with its own risks (the tree could collapse on you or your shelter, the fire could drift and set more of your landscape on fire, etc.). Still, in an extreme emergency, sometimes risks pay off.

For a low-tech and somewhat safer signal, use fabric or plastic ribbons to attract attention to your location. A small mirror is another clever signaling device, and using a mirror to reflect sunlight towards the horizon, or the sky, is surprisingly effective, even over very long distances. In the event that you don't have a mirror, another reflective surface, such as eyeglasses, or a metal pan or spoon, may also work adequately.

The luckiest survivors of all will find themselves on a gorgeous tropical island, where fresh fish and fruit abound, and if needed, the legendary conch shell may be used to blast a note to gather your family together. We're allowed a wee bit of wishful thinking, are we not?

Getting Crafty: Making More From Nature's Bounty

Should you find yourself having an extended wilderness experience, you may wish to pass the time with some useful and creative crafts. Grasses and pine needles are prime materials for basket making, and may also be woven into mats or covers.

You won't find it difficult to make a rudimentary basket, but find instructions on line and include a copy in your regional guide. Similarly, many cultures make earthen bricks, ovens, or receptacles. The adobe tradition (bricks made with sand, clay and water) is alive and well in many southern areas such as New Mexico, but there are other ways of using mud as a creative resource.

Some types of mud are cooling agents and known to have disinfectant properties. What types of mud are found in your area?

Get creative with kindling! Try using pinecones, dried pine needles, moss, and even animal hair to start your wilderness campfire. The drier the materials, the better they will light. Remember that these items will burn very quickly, so have your other fuel handy.

If you are located near a shore, seashells and the shells of crustaceans have many practical uses, as dishes, or crushed and made into a tasty soup stock. They can also hold small candle ends, or be strung together to make a wind chime. Seaweed also has uses beyond plain eating, such as soap making, and composting. Let your imagine explore with you, and make the most of the resources in your landscape.

Final Thoughts: Small Steps, Big Security

Feeling overwhelmed? Don't worry. There is much to be done, but preparing for a crisis is an ongoing project, and not one you can start and finish in a day or week. Any measures you take to observe and explore your natural surroundings will only add to your capacity for survival.

A marker of excellence in terms of preparedness is flexibility. Choose tools and resources that have multiple uses, plan many escape routes, and know how to identify or build shelter under diverse conditions. Share what you learn with friends and loved ones, and exploit the knowledge of your peers. The more confidence in your skills and knowledge about your region you gain, the greater will be your chance to rescue yourself and those you love from disaster.

Good luck, fellow preppers!

*****

If you've enjoyed this book, **please** consider leaving a review and letting others know what you thought!

www.ingramcontent.com/pod-product-compliance
Lightning Source LLC
Chambersburg PA
CBHW070823290526
45795CB00002B/826